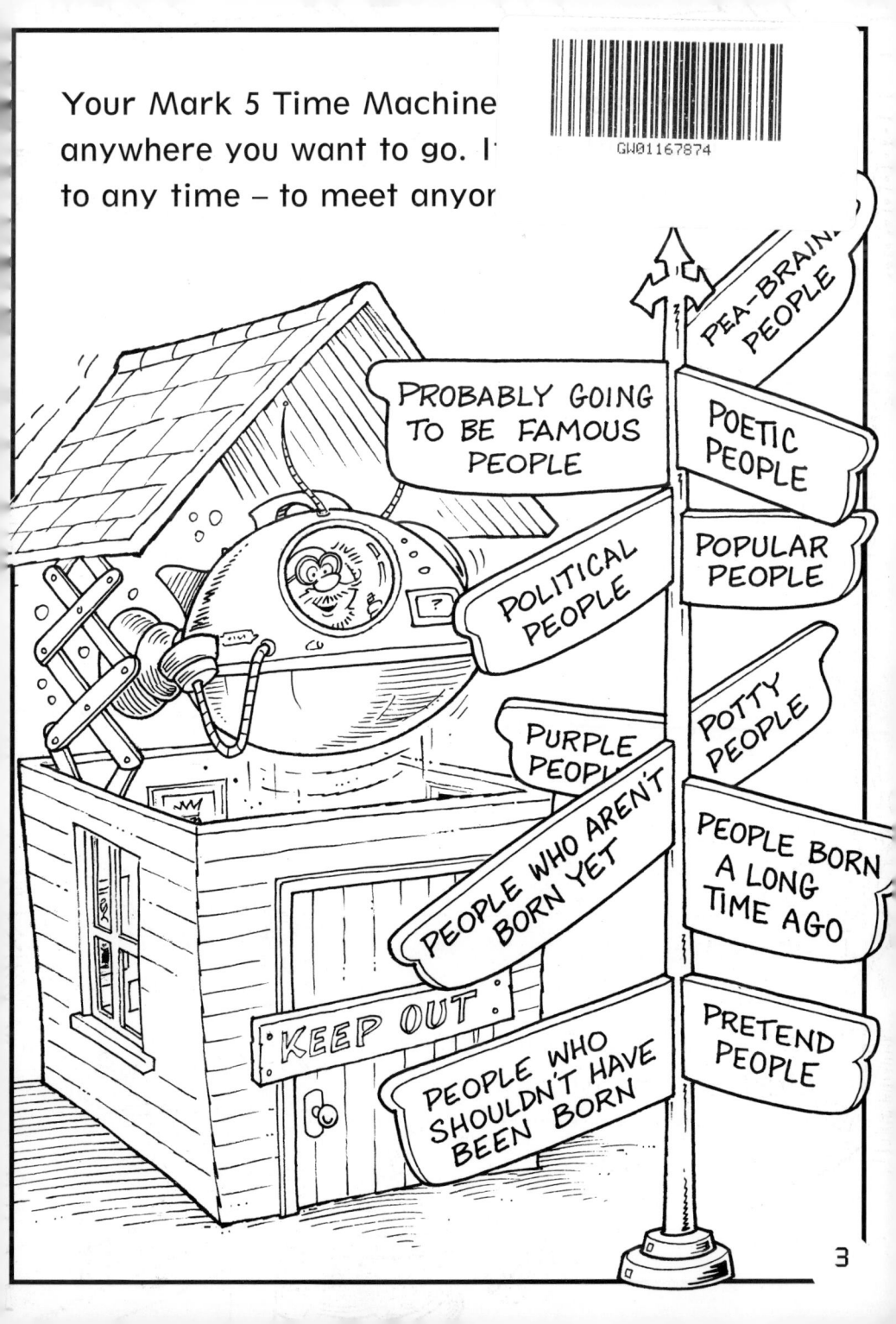

Your Mark 5 Time Machine
anywhere you want to go. I
to any time – to meet anyor

PEA-BRAIN PEOPLE
PROBABLY GOING TO BE FAMOUS PEOPLE
POETIC PEOPLE
POLITICAL PEOPLE
POPULAR PEOPLE
POTTY PEOPLE
PURPLE PEOPL
PEOPLE WHO AREN'T BORN YET
PEOPLE BORN A LONG TIME AGO
KEEP OUT
PEOPLE WHO SHOULDN'T HAVE BEEN BORN
PRETEND PEOPLE

I have met many famous people in my travels. (Or perhaps I should say that many famous people have met me!)

May I have your autograph, please, Mr Zigler?

So here is my latest book: The Anthony J Zigler Guide to Famous People. You can use it to see who you want to go and visit.

Arthur

I met this chap before he became king. He was a nice lad but not very strong.

Thanks, Mr Zigler!

Blackbeard

He was a sweet little baby but not so nice when he grew up. I stopped sending him Christmas cards.

But I used to change your nappies!

Cleopatra

A charming lady. Mrs Zigler was jealous when I told her about our meeting!

Dick Turpin

I wasn't keen on him but his horse was OK.

You are supposed to hold up stagecoaches, you fool – not time machines!

Elvis Presley

I like to think that I helped this young man make it to the top.

Florence Nightingale

I'm always glad to help out when I can ...

Mr Zigler, do you happen to have a match? My lamp has gone out.

Godiva

It was quite a chilly day when I popped back to Coventry to see this lady.

Please borrow my coat, dear lady. You'll catch your death of cold!

12

Henry VIII

Henry was a little careless with wives, so I left Mrs Zigler at home that day.

Indianna Sidebottom

"Who is she?" I hear you ask. She was my great great great grandmother.
She climbed Everest at the age of 97.

Why can't she take up knitting like other old ladies!

Julius Caesar

I like to think I gave this chap a few ideas ...

Personally, Jules, I'd forget invading Ancient Britain if I were you – there's not much in the way of roads or baths ...

15

King Canute

This crazy king had some mad idea to show how powerful he was.

Maybe it might work if we BOTH try?

Long John Silver

I met this man when I followed the Pretend People sign ...

Long John, have you ever thought of having a parrot instead of an ostrich?

Melba

Dame Nellie Melba first appeared in opera in 1887. (I was there.) I liked her so much that I named a pudding after her!

Nelson

Horatio and I often took a boat out together ...

Old Father Time

I know you think he's not real, but he is.
He's alive and well and living on the planet Klok.

Pepys

If it hadn't have been for me, there wouldn't have BEEN any diaries!

Queen Elizabeth II

I popped back through time for her coronation — just to see if there was anything I could do to help.

Robin Hood

I had some good times with Robin and the lads ...

Next time I come, I'll bring some burgers.

TEA TIME 4·30

TOMATO SAUCE

Shakespeare

We writers always try to help each other …

Tutankhamun

I went to see him when he was getting his tomb ready. Boy, did he have some good stuff!

Tutti, you really should think about having a burglar alarm fitted ...

25

Uncle Scoffi

I confess, I told a lie on page 18. It was Uncle Scoffi (better known as Escoffier) who invented the peach melba.

Don't you DARE try pinching my ideas again!

Viking Vera

Viking Vera and her son Erik had this bright idea for holidays ...

...AND you get to stop off in Britain!

But Spain is much warmer ...

LUXURY LONGSHIP CRUISES

PILLAGE TOURS

PLEASE TAKE ONE

CONDITIONS OF SAIL

NO DOGS

27

William Tell

This chap is famous for shooting an apple off his son's head. The trouble is, he couldn't stop doing it after that.

X

X is my mystery famous person.
Can you guess who he is?

I don't know why he did this – I could easily have put my wellies on.

cloak

royal feet

puddle

Young Boudicca

I went to see her when she was just a little girl.

ICENI TEENIES PLAYGROUP

I keep telling her mum not to worry – I'm sure she'll grow out of it.